Virtual Reality Real Estate

Exploring and Investing in the Digital World

Table of Contents

1. Introduction 1

2. The Dawn of Virtual Reality Real Estate 2

    2.1. The Collision of Real Estate and Virtual Reality 2

    2.2. The Intricate Process of Virtual Staging 3

    2.3. The Boon of Virtual Property Viewing 3

    2.4. Profitability in the Digital Real Estate Market 4

    2.5. Future Prospects of Virtual Reality Real Estate 4

3. Understanding the Concept: Virtual Landscapes 6

    3.1. The Genesis of Virtual Landscapes 6

    3.2. Features of Virtual Landscapes 6

    3.3. Virtual Landscapes as Real Estate 7

    3.4. Virtual Landscapes and Blockchain Technology 8

    3.5. Conclusion: Virtual Landscapes & The Future 8

4. The Mechanics of Virtual Realty: A Deep Dive 9

    4.1. Investing in the Intangible 9

    4.2. Ownership and Transactions 10

    4.3. The Immersive Interface - VR Hardware 10

    4.4. The Secure Transaction - Blockchain Technology 11

    4.5. Managing and Improving your Virtual Assets 11

    4.6. Monetizing Virtual Properties 11

    4.7. The Spatial Web and Metaverse 12

    4.8. The Impact of Decentralization 12

5. The Virtual Property Tour: A Revolution in Home Hunting 14

    5.1. The Dawn of Virtual Property Tours 14

    5.2. Financial and Time-Saving Benefits 15

    5.3. Technological Innovations Shaping the Experience 15

    5.4. Sensor Fusion and IoV 16

    5.5. The Future of Virtual Property Tours 16

6. Technology Behind Virtual Reality: Making the Unreal, Real 18

6.1. The Foundation: Software Across the Spectrum 18

6.2. Hardware: The Window to Virtual Worlds 19

6.3. Sensory Perception: A Symphony of Immersion 19

6.4. Challenges and The Future of VR Tech 20

6.5. Wrapping Up 21

7. Investing in Virtual Real Estate: Prospects and Challenges 22

7.1. Understanding Virtual Real Estate Investment 22

7.2. The Potential Rewards 23

7.3. Navigating the Risks and Challenges 23

7.4. Embracing Legal Uncertainties 24

7.5. Sustainability and Growth 24

7.6. Conclusion 25

8. Case Studies: Successful Virtual Real Estate Investments 26

8.1. The Journey of Michael Arrington: A Blockchain Retreat 26

8.2. The Meteoric Rise of Virtual Amsterdam 26

8.3. The Somnium Space Visionaries 27

8.4. Decentraland's Genesis City 27

8.5. Conclusion 28

9. Critical Evaluation: Risks Associated with Virtual Property 29

9.1. Technological Risks 29

9.2. Regulatory Risks 30

9.3. Financial Risks 30

9.4. Social And Ethical Risks 30

10. The Future of Virtual Reality Real Estate: Predictions and

Possibilities 32

10.1. The Current Landscape of Virtual Reality Real Estate 32

10.2. The Transformative Impact of Blockchain and NFTs 33

10.3. The Emergence of Virtual Hotels, Malls, and Art Galleries . . 33

10.4. Forecasting the Economic Impact 34

10.5. The Diverse Investment Opportunities 34

10.6. The Future: Integration with Augmented Reality and IoT . . . 35

11. Getting Started: Your First Step into Virtual Property
Investment 36

11.1. Understanding the Landscape 36

11.2. Types of Virtual Real Estate 36

11.3. The Potential Profitability 37

11.4. Assessing the Current Market 37

11.5. Investing in Virtual Property 37

11.6. Legal and Financial Considerations 38

11.7. Risks of Virtual Property Investment 38

Chapter 1. Introduction

Venture with us into the captivating realm of Virtual Reality Real Estate in our latest Special Report. In an age when technology grants us the ability to explore and build in digital landscapes, this engaging domain is becoming ever more tantalizing for enthusiasts and investors alike. Capturing the essence of this sophisticated blend of the virtual and tangible, our report gently unwraps its complexities, making it effortlessly understandable for everyone. From exploring the intricacies of virtual property visits to diving into the profitability of investing in digital real estate, we've gathered insights from industry experts, successful investors, and techno futurists. This comprehensive Special Report is your compass, your guide, your partner in navigating the world of Virtual Reality Real Estate - a world of endless possibilities and rewarding adventures. Embark on this journey with us, and let's unlock the potentials of this exciting frontier!

Chapter 2. The Dawn of Virtual Reality Real Estate

Historians credit the genesis of real estate transactions with the advent of agriculture. As populations grew and humans recognized the value of owning specific stretches of land and property, they began bartering, buying, and selling dwellings and territories. Since then, the real estate industry has continued to evolve, with digitalization and virtualization being the recent transformative technologies. Today, we stand on the brink of another revolution with Virtual Reality (VR) Real Estate. With the help of VR, investors and ordinary purchasers alike can traverse property from miles away, bypassing geographical constraints, and saving time and resources.

2.1. The Collision of Real Estate and Virtual Reality

Virtual Reality, a technology that immerses users into a computer-generated digital world, presents users with a comprehensive sensory experience. When combined with real estate - a tangible, predominantly physical domain until recently - VR spurs an entirely new way of viewing and conducting property transactions.

The true marvel in the amalgamation of the real estate industry and Virtual Reality lies in the interweaving of physical existence with digital landscapes. Today, with a VR headset and suitable software, a potential buyer in California can tour an apartment in New York or a beach house in Miami, virtually replicating the experience of a physical visit. The rise of VR platforms is now enabling Realtors to showcase properties to clients living in different continents, thereby increasing their client scope and revolutionizing marketing techniques.

2.2. The Intricate Process of Virtual Staging

Virtual Staging, a crucial aspect of Virtual Reality Real Estate, offers an elaborative and immersive experience of a property. It employs a realistic representation of an environment that is yet to be physically built, or a bare property designed and furnished according to a buyer's preference.

With the help of advanced 3D modeling and rendering software, architects and designers model and recreate the proposed construction in a vivid Virtual Reality environment. While the vast majority of this process lies in designing digital models, adding layers of augmented reality animations to stimulate reality presents an extra layer of complexity. This virtually recreated property then provides an aesthetically engaging, authentic experience to potential buyers.

2.3. The Boon of Virtual Property Viewing

Unlike traditionally static images or even a 360-degree photo, a Virtual Reality tour allows buyers to move around the property autonomously. This degree of freedom provides a more genuine and intimate impression of the size, layout, and feel of a property, without having to be physically present.

This interactive, in-depth exploration can offer significant advantages to international buyers. Virtual Reality tours can not only capture the property but can also include surroundings, like streets, parks, and nearby landmarks. This comprehensive viewing experience not only saves travel time and costs, but it also reduces the timeline from the property viewing to the final decision-making process.

2.4. Profitability in the Digital Real Estate Market

The profitability of VR Real Estate operates on the proposed value of digitally created property. While virtual lands do not exist tangibly, they bear real-world value due to their eventual utility, scarcity, and the demand led by tech enthusiasts, investors, and brands.

Investing in digital real estate involves buying pieces of land within VR platforms. In contrast to physical properties, virtual properties offer impressive returns based on their development and popularity. Investors can profit from their virtual holdings by selling them at a higher value, leasing them to other users or commercial entities, or monetizing their use in creative ways, such as by hosting ads or offering subscription-based services.

2.5. Future Prospects of Virtual Reality Real Estate

The shift towards Virtual Reality Real Estate is more than a passing trend. As VR technology continues to evolve, the boundaries between the physical and virtual worlds will become more blurred. Future advancements may allow virtual property visits to become sensorial experiences, allowing prospective buyers to touch, smell, and hear elements of properties they tour — all from the comfort of their living rooms.

Moreover, as our daily activities continue to intermingle with the digital realm, owning digital real estate could potentially offer individuals and companies a way to exist both physically and virtually. Such a phenomenon will bring about considerable changes to the traditional ideas of property, ownership, and existence, catapulting us further into the digital age.

In conclusion, the advent of Virtual Reality Real Estate marks an exciting and revolutionary technological era. While there are still many rivers to cross in VR's journey to mainstream acceptance, the prospects are promising. As we chart our course through this avant-garde technological landscape, one thing is abundantly clear: Virtual Reality Real Estate is here to stay, reshaping our experience of space and property forever.

Chapter 3. Understanding the Concept: Virtual Landscapes

In order to cultivate an understanding of virtual landscapes, it's imperative to frame the contentious yet exhilarating blend of technology, real estate and investment in an immersive, digital environment. These landscapes, often perceived as realms of fantasy, carry authentic weight in the realm of real estate and have evolved into dynamic platforms for innovations and novel opportunities.

3.1. The Genesis of Virtual Landscapes

The inception of virtual landscapes is closely intertwined with the advent and evolution of the Internet. Initially conceived as platforms for experimentation and gaming, these digital spaces gradually matured, mirroring the physical world in terms of communal activities, commerce, and even governance. With advancements in computational power and the evolution of 3D graphics, these landscapes have transformed into highly immersive environments that often blur the lines between the virtual and the physical.

3.2. Features of Virtual Landscapes

Virtual landscapes exhibit a compelling array of features that distinguish them from traditional real-world settings. The core attributes of a virtual landscape include as its immateriality, scalability, customizability, and permanence.

1. **Immateriality**: Virtual landscapes are composed of digital elements and exist entirely within computer systems.

2. **Scalability**: The extent of virtual spaces can be expanded or

contracted with negligible incremental cost.

3. **Customizability**: The appearance and functionality of virtual landscapes can be tailored to meet the specific needs or whims of its owners or visitors.

4. **Permanence**: Despite their immaterial nature, these digital realms persist over time, independent of physical boundaries or regulations.

3.3. Virtual Landscapes as Real Estate

Parallels can be drawn between real-world real estate and virtual landscapes. Both present location-based value, exhibit dimensions of exclusivity, and offer possibilities of infrastructure development.

Location-based value reflects in terms of the proximity to prominent landmarks, commercial hubs or points of interests. While the concept of location in a virtual world might seem intangible, the importance of proximity to high-traffic areas or popular in-world sites cannot be understated.

Exclusivity in owning a piece of digital land can carry as much weight as owning a physical property. Just as each physical plot of land is unique, so too is each parcel in the virtual world, making it an exclusive property of the owner.

Development opportunities in virtual landscapes can potentially outdo physical ones, as the laws of physics do not constrain creativity and ambition.

3.4. Virtual Landscapes and Blockchain Technology

The connection between blockchain and virtual landscapes lies in the proposition of provenance, ownership verification, and transaction security. Blockchain technology enables immutable record-keeping and ensures secure, transparent transactions - pivotal elements for any form of real estate investment.

3.5. Conclusion: Virtual Landscapes & The Future

As the digital age propels forward, we're witnessing global societies evolve into parallel virtual societies. With the ever-increasing integration of virtual landscapes and blockchains, boundaries will further fade, expanding the scope of activities and interactions within these digital realms.

To comprehend virtual landscapes fully, one needs to leave preconceived notions about reality at the door, adopt an open mind, and genuinely attempt to understand and envision the potential of this burgeoning aspect of technology and real estate. Explore, inquire, and invest – the virtual landscapes await your footprints.

Chapter 4. The Mechanics of Virtual Realty: A Deep Dive

Introductory principles of VR Real Estate === The Virtual Landscape

The concept of real estate in the digital realm may seem alien to those accustomed to conventional property investing. Yet in essence, the fundamental principles remain the same, intertwining with the innovative characteristics of the virtual world. Virtual Reality (VR) real estate operates through the medium of digital landscapes, built using graphics rendering software. These landscapes are then imbued with interactivity and functionality through coding within the underlying game engine that houses them. Think of the vast worlds inside video games or the interactive simulations used for training and education. Now imagine owning a piece of that universe; that's the premise of virtual real estate.

4.1. Investing in the Intangible

Despite not being tangible in the traditional sense, digital properties are assets with demand stemming from a variety of sectors. Businesses - both established and startups alike - are exploring the immersive medium of XR (Extended Reality, an umbrella term for VR, AR, and mixed reality) in marketing, training, customer engagement, design, testing, and more. Consumers are also participating in virtual worlds for gaming, socializing, and creating content for digital platforms. The value of virtual properties is determined by the unique aspects they offer, much like physical real estate: location, development potential, desirability, and usage rights play a significant role.

4.2. Ownership and Transactions

Unlike physical property transactions, the acquisition and sale of virtual land occur entirely online. The land deeds are recorded utilising blockchain technology - a distributed, secure digital ledger. Pertaining to the concept of smart contracts, blockchain ensures the property transferred is traced back to the rightful owner, offering an immutable record of the transaction. It provides a level of transparency and security that is rare in the world of digital goods.

Understanding the technology behind VR Real Estate === The Building Blocks - Unity and Unreal Engine

Most virtual spaces are developed using game engines like Unity or Unreal Engine. These powerful software packages allow developers to craft intricate 3D environments complete with physics, lighting, sound, AI, and more. Unity is known for its flexibility and ease of use, while Unreal Engine often excels in delivering high-fidelity graphics.

4.3. The Immersive Interface - VR Hardware

Experiencing these virtual landscapes requires appropriate hardware: primarily headsets such as the Oculus Rift, HTC Vive, or standalone devices like the Oculus Quest. Controllers provide interactivity, simulating hand movements within the virtual environment. Modern VR tech also includes room-scale tracking, which allows users to physically walk around their VR space, and haptic feedback, offering tactile responses to virtual interactions.

4.4. The Secure Transaction - Blockchain Technology

As stated earlier, transactions in the virtual real estate market are securely handled with blockchain technology's help. Blockchain pairs well with virtual real estate due to its core attributes of decentralization and transparency. Transactions are held as records that cannot be tampered with, helping prevent fraud and proving ownership.

Virtual Property Development and Management === Constructing Digital Properties

A virtual property can be as simple as an undeveloped plot of land or as complex as a multipurpose environment with interactive features. Developers build these properties using a 3D modeling program to design and shape the virtual landscape. Once the physical structure is established, they then script various behaviors into the environment such as opening doors or activating lights.

4.5. Managing and Improving your Virtual Assets

The value of virtual properties often increases with improvements and development, just like in physical real estate. Digital property owners are free to hire developers to turn an empty plot into a bustling virtual mall, a stunning art gallery, or a virtual concert space.

4.6. Monetizing Virtual Properties

Monetizing virtual real estate encompasses tactics similar to its tangible counterpart: leasing out virtual land, selling advertising space, charging access to unique experiences, and creating digital goods and services within your property. With the advent of the spatial web (a blend of physical and virtual realities), opportunities to profit from virtual properties will continue to emerge.

Virtual Realty and The Future === Trends in VR Real Estate

From a futurist's perspective, virtual reality real estate follows a trajectory much like the early days of the internet. As technology advances and costs decrease, a rapidly increasing number of users will lead to heightened demand for virtual real estate.

4.7. The Spatial Web and Metaverse

The "Spatial Web" and the "Metaverse" are concepts often discussed in the context of the future of virtual real estate. The Spatial Web refers to the merging of physical and virtual realities. Imagine navigating the internet in a 3D, fully immersive format. The Metaverse, on the other hand, is a universe of interconnected, immersive, expressive virtual spaces. The eventual realization of these concepts has the potential to drive tremendous value in virtual real estate.

4.8. The Impact of Decentralization

Decentralization is another aspect that's profoundly impacting VR real estate. Blockchain technology enables the notion of decentralized virtual worlds - a concept that contrasts with the centralized control seen in traditional MMOs (Massively Multiplayer Online games) and other virtual spaces. Decentralized land ownership empowers user creativity and offers a democratic approach to the future of digital interaction.

To conclude, the complexities of virtual realty are as fascinating as they are intricate. As this domain continues to evolve, it harbors the potential to transform our interactions with the digital arena. This uncharted territory demands exploration as well as strategic investment. The current technological era not only beckons us to adapt to the new but also to become active participants in shaping its future. Virtual Reality Real Estate indeed offers an enticing blend of anticipation and promise for those bold enough to venture into its expansive landscapes.

Chapter 5. The Virtual Property Tour: A Revolution in Home Hunting

In the digital age, the traditional methods of real estate viewing - the physical open houses and property walks have paved way for a more immersive experience through virtual property tours. This profound shift is shaking the very foundations of the real estate industry and redefining the experience of home hunting.

5.1. The Dawn of Virtual Property Tours

Virtual property tours are not a completely new concept. It first saw the light in the mid-90s, when a modest beginning was made through 360-degree photographs and video tours. However, it was the advent of Virtual Reality (VR) technology that gave a remarkable thrust to this paradigm. Today, potential buyers can literally "walk" inside a house, inspecting every nook and corner, without physically stepping into the property.

Such virtual tours are created using sophisticated software that stitches together multiple photos or scans of a property into one interactive 3D model. Users can then don VR goggles, which transport them to the digitized property. It's an incredibly immersive experience - you can open doors, walk through all rooms, check out the views from the windows, and even digitally stage the space with different furniture and décor.

5.2. Financial and Time-Saving Benefits

While the unique and immersive experiences offered by virtual property tours are undeniable, the benefits of this technology extend further. It is a perfect solution for long-distance purchases, as potential buyers can tour properties across the globe at any time of the day. The efficiency and convenience provided by virtual touring is transforming real estate industry's paradigms, making it possible for agents to show dozens of homes in a day without leaving their offices.

From a financial perspective, the capacity to virtually inspect numerous properties allows for a more calculated investment. It significantly decreases the odds of remorseful purchases, as buyers can explore as many properties as they wish before settling on their decision.

5.3. Technological Innovations Shaping the Experience

The technological foundations that make virtual property tours possible are continually being innovated. While the fundamental VR technology has remained the same, the experience is now more intuitive and true-to-life with high definition scanning and rendering.

Furthermore, enhancements like AI-guided tours customize the experience for each viewer. The AI algorithms in the system take into account viewers' interaction with the property during the tour and adapt the staging or highlights features based on user's preferences or behavior.

5.4. Sensor Fusion and IoV

Integration of sensor fusion and Internet of Things also has a considerable influence on the virtual property tour experience. Sensor fusion involves combining positioning data from various sensors to recognize the user's physical actions in the real world and translate them into corresponding maneuvers inside the digitized property.

Meanwhile, the Internet of Virtual Things (IoV) brings to the table the possibility of incorporating advanced aspects of the property such as smart appliances, energy efficiency, and other IoT functionalities into the VR experience.

5.5. The Future of Virtual Property Tours

The future of virtual property tours is set to converge with the development of related technologies. As VR becomes more accessible and affordable, more users will be able to explore properties within this immersive medium.

Moreover, innovations in spatial computing and digital twinning are set to revolutionize the virtual tour experience. Spatial computing enables seamless transitioning between real and virtual spaces, thus enhancing the realism and applicability of these virtual tours. On the other hand, digital twin technology can create highly accurate duplicates of properties for viewing, which can be updated in real time as changes are made to the original property.

To sum up, the revolution in home hunting brought about by virtual property tours is just the beginning. As technology continues to evolve, the real estate industry should be prepared for an even greater transformation. This digital shift not only increases accessibility and convenience but is also set to drastically change the way we understand and perceive real estate. Technology is steadily altering the very paradigms of the real estate industry, making it simpler, wider, and more inclusive.

Chapter 6. Technology Behind Virtual Reality: Making the Unreal, Real

The magic of Virtual Reality (VR) is built upon the meticulously choreographed interplay of software, hardware and human sensory perception.

6.1. The Foundation: Software Across the Spectrum

At the heart of VR developments lie powerful engines responsible for creating immersive 3D environments. Two of the most commonly used engines are the Unity3D and Unreal Engine. These platforms enable developers to craft detailed, realistic scenarios that users can interact with in real-time.

Unity3D, known for its user-friendly tools and extensive script library, has contributed to some of the most well-known VR applications today. Coupled with C# as its main programming language, it provides developers with a high-performance rendering pipeline, ideal for creating sophisticated VR simulations.

Unreal Engine, on the other hand, stands out with its advanced lighting systems and realistic physics capability. Primarily utilizing C++, it's preferred by developers for highly detailed and visually demanding projects.

Both engines have democratized VR development, allowing even novice programmers to build interactive 3D worlds, thereby swiftly expanding the VR landscape.

6.2. Hardware: The Window to Virtual Worlds

Hardware acts as the gateway to the VR experience. It consists of Head-Mounted Displays (HMDs), input devices, and tracking systems. Several major tech companies have developed HMDs, each with its unique features.

Oculus, acquired by Facebook (now Meta), offers a flagship product, the Oculus Quest 2. This standalone HMD has in-built sensors for positional tracking and doesn't require a tethering to a high-end PC, breaking barriers to entry.

HTC's Vive Pro Eye distinguishes itself with eye-tracking functionality. Using foveated rendering, it lowers the graphics resources needed by focusing on rendering where the user's gaze lies.

PlayStation VR primarily caters to the console gaming community, boasting a range of compatibility with PlayStation games, thus attracting a significant user base.

Input devices such as hand controllers and haptic gloves are vitally essential for the user to interact with the VR environments. Companies like Oculus and HTC offer proprietary hand controllers, while more specialized companies, like Manus, develop wearable trackers and haptic gloves, providing a more tactile and immersive experience.

6.3. Sensory Perception: A Symphony of Immersion

The success of VR hinges on its ability to convince human senses that digital experiences are real – a phenomenon known as presence. To achieve this, the system orchestrates a symphony between what our eyes see, what our ears hear, and how our bodies move.

Visual cues, delivered via the HMD, are the most obvious players. However, audio plays an equally important role in producing spatial awareness. This technique, known as spatial or 3D sound, makes the environment appear more immersive and real.

Moreover, the sense of motion and position in space, also known as proprioception, is critical. Tracking systems monitor the user's head and body movements and adjust the visual display accordingly. This consistency between motion and visual perception bolsters the sense of presence.

Haptics, another critical component, provides tactile feedback mimicking real contact with virtual objects. This is where VR gloves and suits come into play, offering experiences that go beyond visual and auditory stimuli.

6.4. Challenges and The Future of VR Tech

While VR technology has come a long way, it is not without challenges. Foremost is 'simulation sickness,' caused by the discrepancy between visual motion cues and physical ones, often leading to nausea. Addressing this issue, developments in adaptive algorithms are designed to minimize such inconsistencies.

There's also the continued effort to make VR hardware more affordable, accessible, and comfortable. Future tech potentially could see lightweight glasses replacing bulky headsets, making prolonged use more feasible.

Cloud-based VR is another promising frontier. By offloading processing tasks to cloud servers, high-quality VR experiences could be delivered even on lower-end hardware, vastly democratizing access to VR.

6.5. Wrapping Up

The fabrication of virtual reality is an incredible example of technology's power to bridge the gap between the tangible and the conceptual. The journey from basic software architecture to perception manipulation showcases how far we've come, and hints at how much farther we could go in the spectrum of digital experience. As we continue to improve upon these systems, the promise of fully immersive, indistinguishable digital realities becomes increasingly palpable.

It's not difficult to imagine a future where, aided by VR, the transition from a physical to a digital space feels as natural as walking from one room into another. This technology offers the intriguing potential of Virtual Reality Real Estate, turning what was once a science fiction dream into a practical, profitable reality. Yet, there's a frontier of possibilities just starting to unfold. As the technologies continue to evolve, so too will the ways we interact with, and within, virtual spaces.

Chapter 7. Investing in Virtual Real Estate: Prospects and Challenges

Just as in the traditional real estate sector, investing in virtual real estate offers intriguing avenues for profit, coupled with its own unique set of challenges.

7.1. Understanding Virtual Real Estate Investment

Virtual real estate refers to digital land that forms part of a completely virtual world. These properties exist within multiple platforms, including games like Minecraft or Second Life, as well as purpose-built environments like Decentraland and Cryptovoxels, blockchain-based virtual worlds where land is permanently owned by the buyer. While investments in virtual properties were initially a niche interest, the expansion of virtual reality and blockchain technologies has brought a surge of interest, and with it, surge in value.

Investing in digital real estate can be approached in multiple ways. Perennial methods include buying low and selling high, renting your virtual properties, or monetizing them through various forms of advertising. Some investors have made a considerable fortune simply by snapping up early parcels in now-popular virtual worlds. However, as the market matures, we're also seeing more sophisticated strategies evolved, such as the development of virtual commercial properties or tourist destinations.

7.2. The Potential Rewards

Potential rewards abound in the world of virtual real estate. Rapid technological advances, combined with increasing acceptance and use of cryptocurrency, have made digital assets more attractive. High-profile purchases, such as the recent sale of a virtual property for approximately $500,000 in the Ethereum equivalent, have grabbed international headlines and demonstrated the increasing value attached to these novel properties.

At the same time, the barriers to entry for virtual real estate investment are significantly lower than their physical counterparts. Virtual properties are typically much less expensive, especially in newer or less-known environments. Similarly, the costs and complexities associated with property maintenance, taxes, and legal work in the physical world are largely absent from the virtual.

Monetization of digital real estate is also growing, both in scope and sophistication. Methods now extend beyond simple advertising to include transaction fees, hosting virtual events, or creating in-demand virtual experiences.

7.3. Navigating the Risks and Challenges

Though the prospects are alluring, investing in virtual real estate also comes with notable risks and challenges. For newcomers especially, getting to grips with the foundational technology, such as blockchain and virtual reality, can be daunting.

The volatility of cryptocurrency, which is often the medium of exchange for these properties, can turn would-be gains into sudden losses. It can also swing the other way - properties purchased for a relative steal can become highly valuable overnight.

One fundamental challenge is that virtual worlds are typically owned by private entities. While blockchain provides a degree of certainty in ownership, the world itself is dependent on the server it's hosted on - and the company that owns those servers. In theory, a virtual world and all properties within it could disappear tomorrow, if the hosting company folds or decides to discontinue the world.

7.4. Embracing Legal Uncertainties

Regulations and legal frameworks around virtual property rights remain scant across the globe. Though traditional real estate is heavily governed by a complex system of laws and regulations, no such system exists in the virtual world. Property rights, dispute resolution, regulations against fraud, are either absent, or their application to digital properties is untested. This presents a significant risk for heavy investment until clear regulations are established.

7.5. Sustainability and Growth

While the concept of virtual real estate has existed for over a decade, more recent developments in technology have propelled it into the mainstream. Investment in virtual real estate is undoubtedly on an upward trajectory. However, questions about how sustainable this growth is remain. Is it a bubble, or is it here to stay?

The technology underpinning virtual real estate – principally blockchain and virtual reality – are themselves subject to shifts and changes. Those who are considering investing will want to keep a close eye on these technologies, the trends shaping them, and their potential impact.

7.6. Conclusion

Virtual reality real estate holds appeal for those who are technically-savvy, forward-thinking, and accepting of a level of risk. It's an intriguing realm - offering a blend of opportunities from asset appreciation to creative expression. For those who understand the fundamentals of blockchain and virtual reality, and who are willing to navigate the potential challenges, there are ample opportunities for investment and growth. However, as with any pioneering frontier, it is crucial to tread cautiously as the territory is still being discovered, with regulatory protections notably absent and technological uncertainties still playing out.

Chapter 8. Case Studies: Successful Virtual Real Estate Investments

For those venturing into the world of virtual reality real estate, it can be most enlightening to study the achievements of those who have already found success in this dynamic field. With each case offering its own unique insights, we explore the fertile landscapes of virtual real estate through the journeys of those who dared to delve, create, invest, and ultimately prosper.

8.1. The Journey of Michael Arrington: A Blockchain Retreat

When TechCrunch founder Michael Arrington invested in a piece of virtual real estate on Ethereum blockchain, many eyebrows were raised. The property, located within the virtual landscape of Decentraland, was purchased with cryptocurrency, and turned heads in both the virtual reality and real estate sectors.

Arrington managed to secure the property for around $20,000 US equivalent. Observers watched cautiously, wondering if this investment could genuinely hold the potential for return. As it turns out, it did. Arrington's virtual property has since skyrocketed in value, with similar properties now commanding prices exceeding $200,000.

8.2. The Meteoric Rise of Virtual Amsterdam

Famed in the virtual world, Virtual Amsterdam stands as an

exemplar of a successful investment within the pioneering platform, Second Life. It was created as an exact replica of the Dutch capital. Initially purchased for a modest sum in Second Life's in-world currency, the landmark city has since generated substantial profits through virtual tourism, property rentals, virtual good sales, and more.

It's been a venture that has transcended classic virtual boundaries and emerged as a lucrative destination in itself, attracting countless visitors who want to explore Amsterdam from their living rooms and offering in-world inhabitants a place to live, right at the heart of virtual Europe.

8.3. The Somnium Space Visionaries

In Somnium Space, a virtual reality world on the Ethereum blockchain, investors see another incredible tale unravel. The vast, immersive platform allows users to purchase land, build upon it, and then resell or rent it out at a profit.

A fine example is an investor who took the plunge to buy several waterfront properties early on. The investor made the strategic choice, under the belief that properties with unique features or appealing views would appreciate more. The bold vision paid off exponentially when the value of these properties ballooned with the growing interest in VR real estate. As Somnium Space's popularity surged, so too did the worth of the virtual properties, yielding remarkable returns for their strategic owners.

8.4. Decentraland's Genesis City

Yet another case worth discussing is Genesis City in Decentraland. A fully decentralized city, where LAND (the non-fungible, transferable, scarce digital asset held in an Ethereum smart contract) can be purchased.

Early adopters who bought LAND parcels have reaped significant benefits from their prime location purchases. These parcels were bought for fractions of Ether (ETH), but several have been sold for upwards of hundreds of thousands of dollars, marking some of the highest profitable turnovers in virtual real estate history.

8.5. Conclusion

The future looks bright -and quite profitable - for virtual reality real estate. As these case studies illustrate, savvy investors and visionaries who understood the potential of blending the digital and tangible worlds reaped significant rewards.

There are several lessons to be gleaned from their experiences. Key among them is the ability to recognize and seize unique opportunities, being strategic about location selection, and understanding the value that other virtual dwellers may assign to certain property features. Importantly, as virtual reality technology advances, we could witness even more incredible growth in this field.

Indeed, while this new form of real estate might still feel otherworldly to some, for those brave enough to step into the digital landscape, the rewards could be virtually limitless.

Chapter 9. Critical Evaluation: Risks Associated with Virtual Property

In the enthusiasm encompassing the realm of Virtual Reality Real Estate, it is essential not to overlook the key factor of risk. Before diving head-first into the exciting possibilities that this technology promises, we must critically evaluate the potential issues that might emerge in this virtual yet tangible realm.

9.1. Technological Risks

At its core, virtual real estate is powerfully reliant on technology. This, by default, implies a set of substantial risks. Here are some of the most pressing concerns:

- Technological Instability: Virtual Reality (VR) landscapes are intricate, technology-driven environments. The fragility of such sophistication leads to an unavoidable probability of technical glitches, crashes or complete system failure, which can interrupt property viewing or transactions. In severe cases, a technical downfall might result in the loss of property data, thus impacting the value of the investment.

- Cybersecurity Threats: Like any digital asset, virtual real estate is susceptible to cyber attacks such as hacking, fraud, and identity theft. While most platforms ensure top-notch security measures, the risk, however minimal, still exists.

- Obsolescence Risk: Given the rapid pace at which tech evolves, there's always a chance that the platform your virtual property is on could become obsolete. This could devalue your property or even render it useless.

9.2. Regulatory Risks

Governments and regulatory bodies have yet to catch up with the advancements of virtual reality and virtual real estate industry. This leads to a set of regulatory risks:

- Undefined Legal Framework: Virtual real estate currently resides in a sort of legal "wild west" with no specific framework to govern it. Ownership, taxation, dispute resolution and property rights are all uncharted territories that pose a significant risk.

- Future Legislation: The current legal vacuum means that future legislation could go in any direction, either benefiting or harming investors. Such uncertainty makes the risk factor high.

9.3. Financial Risks

While the prospect of earning significant returns in virtual real estate is appealing, potential financial risks need to be taken into account:

- Volatility: The value of virtual real estate echoes the volatility of its cousin, cryptocurrency. As the market fluctuates, so does the value of your property.

- Illiquidity: Depending on the platform, reselling virtual properties might be easier said than done. This could tie down your investment in an undesirable manner.

9.4. Social And Ethical Risks

In addition to the aforementioned risks, there are several social and ethical risks, often overlooked, associated with investing in virtual real estate:

- Property Misuse: Virtual environments provide anonymity,

which can potentially lead to misuse of property. Property owners may find their spaces used for illicit activities, without any real mechanism for control or redress.

- Accessibility Issues: Virtual real estate could widen the gap between the digital haves and have-nots. The high costs of technology required might exclude certain sections of society from enjoying or using these spaces.

In summary, investing in the world of virtual real estate requires a balanced outlook – a well-rounded understanding of both the exciting prospects and significant risks it entails. The thrill of pioneering into a new domain is attractive, but it is equally important to critically evaluate the potential pitfalls. Future growth and stability in the realm of Virtual Reality Real Estate will largely depend on how these risks are navigated and managed. As we venture further into this realm, investors must harness caution as much as they harness their vision.

Adopting a realistic, well-informed approach to the path ahead will ensure that virtual real estate's fantastic potential can be tapped into while minimizing the accompanying risks. Those who accomplish this will truly master this exciting new frontier.

Chapter 10. The Future of Virtual Reality Real Estate: Predictions and Possibilities

Over the past few years, real estate has crossed into the digital realm, creating an entirely new market of virtual real estate. Just as we've seen a boom in the physical property market, the virtual world is experiencing its expansion, powered by a new generation of technology and backed by both individual and corporate investors alike. This layer of 'reality' is in symbiosis with the tangible world, and in some startling ways, has started to outpace it. As we venture further into this digital frontier, let's navigate the possibilities and predictions of this burgeoning phenomenon.

10.1. The Current Landscape of Virtual Reality Real Estate

In the wake of the COVID-19 pandemic, the adoption of Virtual Reality (VR) technology saw a significant increase as people sought new ways to inspect properties without leaving their homes. This provided a fertile ground for the growth of VR in real estate, reaching beyond a simple tool for property viewings into a new investment avenue.

Platforms like Decentraland, Cryptovoxels, and Somnium Space are paving the way for virtual land ownership, powered by blockchain technology. These digital landscapes offer a sandbox for creativity and commerce, granting both owners and visitors the opportunities to build, explore, play games, and conduct business. Within these metaverses, participants can buy, sell, and trade virtual land like physical real estate, complete with deeds recorded on blockchain networks. Enthusiasts and entrepreneurs are expeditiously capitalizing on these digital landscapes, leading to a real estate boom within the confines of VR.

10.2. The Transformative Impact of Blockchain and NFTs

Blockchain, along with its quintessential avatar, Non-Fungible Tokens (NFTs), has flooded into the mainstream over the past years. This technology is playing a transformative role in carving out the VR real estate niche. NFTs are unique digital assets that are indivisible and verifiable, which makes them perfect for representing ownership of unique pieces of property, including parcels of land in the virtual world.

For instance, Decentraland's LAND tokens, an NFT that represents the virtual parcel of land within the platform, can be bought, sold, or traded like any other tangible property. The ownership and transactional details are stored on a blockchain, providing an unprecedented level of transparency and security. This digital ownership model revolutionizes how we perceive and handle assets, bridging the gap between the physical and the virtual.

10.3. The Emergence of Virtual Hotels, Malls, and Art Galleries

In the VR domain, digital locations have emerged as more than just places for recreation or residency, but as thriving commercial hubs. Marketplaces, art galleries, and even cinemas have been created on virtual land, attracting users from all across the globe.

Virtual hotels and malls are not just speculative projections; they are current realities. Metaverses are introducing a new concept of tourism where people can visit and experience different locations from the comfort of their homes. Art galleries are hosting exhibitions from contemporary artists, opening up a new landscape for creative individuals to display and sell their work. The potential for economic activity in VR is alluring, beckoning investors across industries.

10.4. Forecasting the Economic Impact

While still in its infancy, the financial potential of virtual real estate is vast. The global Ar/VR market in real estate was valued at USD 1.07 billion in 2020 and is estimated to reach around USD 4.5 billion by 2025, according to a report by ResearchandMarkets.com.

Large corporations are catching wind of the possibilities that Virtual Reality real estate offers. Industry giants are buying up virtual lands for commercial purposes, and major virtual festivals like the Budweiser event in Decentraland attract thousands of visitors. The popularity of these events and the opportunity for exposure to large audiences can drive the price and value of virtual land upwards.

10.5. The Diverse Investment Opportunities

Virtual Reality is lowering the barriers to real estate investment, allowing a broader demographic to partake. In the real world, real estate investment typically requires significant capital, but in the virtual realm, parcels of land can be bought and sold for less. Furthermore, the potential for virality in VR platforms exposes these properties to a global audience, potentially accelerating returns for savvy investors.

That being said, virtual real estate is not immune to the economic mechanics of the traditional market. Location, proximity to popular attractions, and the potential for development all play a role in the valuation of virtual parcels. Thus, the principles of real estate investment, including market analysis and careful planning, still hold true in the VR domain.

10.6. The Future: Integration with Augmented Reality and IoT

As technology continues to advance, we can expect VR real estate to integrate with other emerging innovations. Augmented Reality (AR) and Internet of Things (IoT) may converge with VR, offering a blend of experiences that intermingle physical and virtual environments. Smart homes could potentially be managed at a distance using VR interfaces on virtual property. The integration of these technologies could herald a new era of hybrid reality, adding a multidimensional layer to our existence.

In conclusion, the future of Virtual Reality real estate sits at the crossroad of innovation and adaptation, driven by the vision of technologists, the creativity of developers, and the appetite of investors. It's an exploration of a new realm, a new way of thinking about space, ownership, and community. The vast, still-untapped potential of this frontier whispers predictions of a future replete with endless possibilities and vast fortunes, vanquishing the bounds of physicality in favor of boundless imagination. Through this lens, we can truly begin to see the future of real estate not just as a place on a map, but a realm within our virtual grasp.

Chapter 11. Getting Started: Your First Step into Virtual Property Investment

As you take your first step into the illustrative realm of Virtual Reality Real Estate investment, it's essential to understand the landscape's basics. We've compiled a comprehensive, step-by-step guide to assist you in your journey. Let's dive right in!

11.1. Understanding the Landscape

Virtual Reality Real Estate, often referred to as VR Real Estate, has made its grand entrance into the property market. It is a digital universe of real estate where anyone can buy, sell, or auction virtual land using in-game currency or authentic-world money. VR Real Estate platforms are often built using blockchain technology, ensuring secure digital ownership that can't be altered or confiscated.

11.2. Types of Virtual Real Estate

Virtual Real Estate can broadly be categorized into two types.

1. Virtual Reality Platforms like Second Life, VR Chat, and Roblox, where users can own lands, create, and sell experiences.

2. Blockchain-based platforms like Decentraland, Cryptovoxels, and Somnium Space. Here, land ownership is represented by non-fungible tokens (NFTs) ensuring provable scarcity and true ownership.

11.3. The Potential Profitability

The potential profitability of investing in virtual real estate is enormous. Comparisons are often drawn between the nascent virtual property market and the early days of the internet. It's a new frontier, and early adopters could potentially reap huge returns. While one might instinctively dismiss virtual lands as 'not real', remember that scarcity drives value. Because blockchain ensures the scarcity of virtual properties, this 'unreal' market demonstrates real economic behaviors.

11.4. Assessing the Current Market

Before you invest, it's crucial to assess the current market. Consider factors such as the popularity of the platform, the demand for virtual land, and the transaction volume. Social media, online communities, and virtual real estate trading platforms are excellent resources for insights. Most importantly, be on the lookout for trends. A sudden influx of users into a platform, for example, could signify a good investment opportunity.

11.5. Investing in Virtual Property

Investing in virtual property is much like investing in physical real estate, with due diligence being a core tenet. Here are some steps:

1. **Research**: Explore various platforms to understand their mechanics and user base.

2. **Budgeting**: Decide your budget based on factors like quantity vs quality (do you buy large swaths of cheap land or a single prime property?)

3. **Evaluate**: Determine the value of a property. Check its location, nearby attractions, and 'foot traffic.'

4. **Purchase**: Once you've found your perfect plot, the purchase process often involves bidding in an auction or buying directly from the platform or other users.

5. **Maximize Value**: It's not just about buying; it's also about what you do with your land. Develop it - virtual concerts, art galleries, games, and virtual stores are just some of the possibilities.

11.6. Legal and Financial Considerations

Virtual property investment represents a new field for both regulatory and tax authorities. Though it is a reality in the digital world, it is nascent in the legal one. It's advisable to engage with a financial advisor versed in digital assets or a legal consultant with knowledge in the tech sphere. Be sure you understand the tax implications of your virtual transactions, particularly if you plan to convert virtual earnings into real-world currency.

11.7. Risks of Virtual Property Investment

As with any investment, understanding the risks is paramount. These can be:

1. Market Volatility: The value of digital real estate can fluctuate wildly.

2. Platform Risks: If the platform you've invested in folds or sees a significant decrease in users, your investment potentially devalues.

3. Regulatory Risks: The legal landscape could change, affecting the value or legality of owned properties.

Having taken this formidable first step, you are now ready to enter the vast untapped vistas of Virtual Reality Real Estate. While the journey might be unpredictable, the destination could be profitable. The key is to approach it with an open mind and a knowledgeable strategy. Happy investing in your virtual future!